DOROTHY ATKINSON

The End of the Russian Land Commune 1905-1930

Stanford University Press, Stanford, California 1983

Stanford University Press
Stanford, California
© 1983 by the Board of Trustees of the
Leland Stanford Junior University
Printed in the United States of America
ISBN 0-8047-1148-8
LC 81-84457

The End of the Russian Land Commune
1905-1930